# When a medical skin condition affects the way you look

## A guide to managing your future

*Changing Faces is a national charity committed to providing help and support for children, their families and adults who have disfigurements, as well as working for better health care and raising public awareness*

**Changing Faces**
**1-2 Junction Mews**
**London W2 1PN**

**Telephone: 020 7706 4232**
**Fax: 020 7706 4234**
**Email: info@changingfaces.co.uk**
**Web: www.changingfaces.co.uk**

**Registered Charity No. 1011222**

*Changing Faces is very grateful for the generous support of GlaxoSmithKline plc in producing this booklet*

*Changing Faces would like to thank the following people for their valuable ideas and contributions: Dr Anthony Bewley, Dr Nichola Rumsey, Mrs Maxine Whitton and the Changing Faces team.*

*Cover illustrations: Gary Embury*
*Design: Binding Associates*
*Print: Taylor Brothers, Bristol*

*ISBN 1 900928 15 9*

# When a medical skin condition affects the way you look

## A guide to managing your future

CONTENTS

# Introduction

Having a medical skin condition* that affects your appearance can be distressing. You may sometimes find it difficult to feel good about yourself and to deal with other people's reactions. If you have a noticeable medical skin condition, especially if it affects your face, this Guide will enable you to face your future with more confidence.

The Guide aims to:
- explore the social and emotional concerns that you may have because of a medical skin condition
- introduce some positive strategies for managing these issues
- signpost you to relevant sources of information, advice and support.

There are hundreds of medical conditions that can affect the appearance of the skin. The most commonly known ones are acne, eczema, psoriasis, vitiligo, birthmarks, neurofibromatosis, scars and burns. The Guide does not aim to give advice, opinions or information of a medical nature. You are strongly urged to contact appropriate medical sources of general and specific information about your individual needs. Details of some of these sources are given at the end of this Guide.

The introductory chapter looks at why having a medical skin condition can be challenging. Chapter Two seeks to help you to dispel the myths about medical skin conditions and develop your attractiveness. Chapter Three advises on how to find good general information and how to contact sources of treatment, advice and support. Chapter Four suggests ways of facing other people with confidence, a crucial aspect of managing your future if you have a medical skin condition. Chapter Five lists helpful organisations related to specific conditions.

* We have used the term 'medical skin condition' in this Guide to refer to the way in which a skin disorder or disease can alter the colour, complexion or pigment of the skin.

With today's preoccupation with appearance, you might feel at a distinct disadvantage if you have a medical skin condition. However, this Guide aims to show you that there is much more to attractiveness than a flawless skin. Being attractive to other people relies on much more important things that you can develop to your advantage – not least your ability to manage your encounters with other people.

# 1. Why our skin matters

## The importance of our skin

Most of us remember from our school lessons that skin is the largest organ of the body, and that it protects you from bacterial infection and the harsh effects of the environment. It also regulates our body temperature, and gives us our important sense of touch. Despite these impressive functions, there are times when we can all feel distressed by our skin.

The skin has many associations – throughout history, for example, there has been much prejudice, intolerance and aggression among some people towards those of a different race, based on skin colour. Emotion is also strongly linked to the touch and feel of skin. And because of the skin's close connections with the nervous system, it is also sensitive to emotional events. It turns pale and clammy when we experience fear (the 'cold sweat' of anxiety), it flushes when we feel embarrassed and it appears to glow when we are happy. Temperature causes reactions too, from reddening and perspiration in the heat to 'goose pimples' and raised hair when cold. People with some skin conditions report that their symptoms get worse during times of stress, tiredness or hormonal change. Sun tan is another way in which some people use their skin to make them feel attractive and healthy despite the fact that it is known to cause signs of ageing and increased risk of skin cancer.

Our skin can convey much about our general health, and certain diseases such as measles, mumps or chickenpox produce characteristic rashes and irritation. The diagnosis of the potentially fatal disease meningitis often rests on the investigation of the accompanying skin rash. Disease of the liver can sometimes be suspected from a yellowing of the skin colour. Allergic reactions are often shown via a skin rash or swelling. In contrast, a clear complexion is believed to give the impression to others of good health.

## Beliefs about the skin and its condition

As we all know, appearances can be deceptive. Sometimes people can get the wrong impression about our skin. Some people believe that conditions such as acne or psoriasis are the result of poor eating patterns or inadequate washing regimes. Modern research shows that although a balanced diet is essential for all aspects of health, these assumptions are incorrect. Similarly, the idea of 'uncleanness' associated with skin disease is without factual basis. Another assumption is that skin conditions are transmissible from one person to another, and that therefore it is necessary to keep a distance. Again, this is incorrect – most medical conditions affecting the skin are not contagious.

## The skin's contribution to beauty

Many people equate a clear skin with what is considered to be beautiful – a characteristic which is highly valued, and considered, in some people's minds, to be almost the same thing as attractiveness. Advertisements, for example, typically assert that, after a makeover, a woman now feels happier with herself. The truth is that if we think we look good, then we tend to feel more confident.

For someone with a medical skin condition, the pervasive messages of advertising can be hard to counter because they can quite wrongly make you think that your skin makes you inferior or unacceptable. This assumption is strengthened in the artificial ways that the film industry uses medical skin conditions as devices to identify characters who are uncontrolled, unkempt or immoral in some way. Monsters, evil witches and ne-er do wells almost always have scars and warty complexions – recent examples include Gary Oldman's multilated face in Hannibal and the Two Face character in the Batman movies.

# 2. Thinking and feeling attractive

## Dispelling the myths

It is not surprising given all the misleading messages in advertising, films and the media, that people who have a medical skin condition can tend to feel that their appearance is off-putting to others, and furthermore that it may spoil their chances of success and happiness. This, in turn can affect what they do and how they behave in company.

The reality is that there are a lot of myths surrounding medical skin conditions, their causes and their treatment. And it is vital that you know how to dispel the myths – not just for yourself but for others too. To do this, it is important to equip yourself with good information about your condition (see Chapter Three for details on getting the facts). But it is also essential for you to dispel the myths in your own thinking.

***Myth one: your skin condition is a result of poor hygiene and haphazard habits.***

This is factually incorrect. In former times it was thought that conditions such as acne arose because of 'dirt getting into the pores' and the cosmetics industry has fed this illusion to some extent. You can help to dispel this myth with your friends and acquaintances but with strangers too, not only by telling them but by showing them.

You can do this by looking after your appearance and personal care at all times. You do not need to wear expensive designer clothing to look smart – just wearing items that are well cared for and appropriate for the occasion will give a good impression. Not only that, but knowing that you have dressed well will work wonders for your self-confidence too.

***Myth two: your skin condition is a result of a poor diet.***

There is plenty of evidence to show that a poor diet does not directly contribute to a poor complexion. Medical skin conditions arise for more complex reasons than this. The assumption prevails nevertheless that there is a simple equation between eating bad food and having bad skin. If you consider your health as a whole though, it does make perfect sense that you owe it to yourself to eat a good varied diet containing all the necessary nutrients and a minimum of 'junk', empty calories and additives. A healthy eating pattern with plenty of vegetables, fruits and fibre will benefit your health in all sorts of ways.

*Myth three: medical skin conditions can be 'catching'.*
Only a minority of medical skin conditions can be transmissible – for example, impetigo. It is essential to seek reliable medical advice regarding such conditions. (See Chapter Three.) Infections can also be transmitted by blood. If you have a sore that is bleeding, seek medical advice immediately regarding its management. If you have a sore, there may be the potential for transmission of bacteria and infection. It is important that you ask for advice about your particular condition from a reliable source of information.

But most medical skin conditions are not transmissible, and it is important to be well equipped with correct information in case you are challenged, or if you want to discuss your condition with other people. The calm presentation of facts is usually the best way to dispel this myth once and for all.

*Myth four: people with medical skin disorders won't find love and romance.*
This myth is perpetuated by fiction, where the heroes and heroines always look perfect and find true romance. The reality is different. Making good friends and having intimate relationships does not require perfect good looks. It does require the ability to be a good friend, having qualities such as friendliness, being loyal, being good fun and supporting others. There are many people who have medical skin conditions who lead very active and successful lives in the romantic sense.

## Thinking positively about attractiveness

Knowing that the myths are myths is one thing but successfully living with a medical skin condition can often mean changing the way you think about attractiveness.

Sometimes, people with a medical skin condition can think that they are defined by their skin. The thought of meeting other people can appear impossible because you are overcome by fears of what they will think of you, and by embarrassment about your skin. It is possible to get this out of all proportion and imagine that your skin condition is somehow responsible for every rebuff and every social failure ever experienced.

This sort of exaggerated thinking is seriously flawed. Other similarly unhelpful patterns of thought include:

- Rejecting good feedback from other people. This means that if someone compliments or praises you, you discount it as being not truthful. (eg: you may think, 'She only invited me out for a meal because she felt sorry for me.')
- Filtering. This involves thinking that people must be thinking badly of you, even when there is no such evidence. (eg: you may think, 'She must be thinking how awful my rash always looks.') These thoughts can often contain extreme language such as always, never ever, nobody, totally.
- Blaming yourself. If someone behaves badly, you may be tempted to think that you are somehow to blame. Conversely, you may feel responsible for making things better single-handedly if things go wrong. (eg: you may think, 'Mike left the party early. It must have been something I did to upset him. I'd better apologise to him.')
- Making a catastrophe out of a challenge. This means predicting a complete disaster will follow a set-back. (eg: you may think, 'If I don't do well with this presentation, then I shall never be able to show my face at work again.')
- 'If only' thinking. It can be tempting sometimes to imagine that if only you did not have your medical skin condition, then everything in life would fall into place with ease. Only the skin condition is holding you back, but as you have it, you may as well not bother to try. If you had a clear healthy skin, then you would be dating the person of your dreams, you would get that top job, or be the most popular student at college… This just does not happen. An honest appraisal of all the clear-skinned people you know will confirm this.

Finding positive ways of thinking about yourself is important if you are to strengthen your self-esteem and self-confidence. If you found the above points familiar, it is time to question your reasoning.

For example, instead of jumping to the conclusion 'They all think I look terrible because I have acne', it is better to ask yourself, 'How do I know what they are thinking?' and then realise that your original conclusion may have just been guesswork on your part. You are probably not any less attractive than the others you are worrying about. It is quite possible that people are not judging, evaluating or even noticing you very much. Perhaps they are even thinking about their own appearance.

New ways of thinking positively about situations can be encouraged if you use the sort of compassionate understanding and supportive approaches that you would use if you were helping someone else.

## Looking attractive

Not only is it possible to think positively about your appearance if you have a medical skin condition; it is also important to pay considerable attention to your physical appearance, not just your face of course, and here are some tips for looking attractive:

● Make sure you are well-presented with tidy clothes, clean finger nails and hair. Take care to do this thoroughly but do not become obsessive. Play to your strengths. If you think you have nice hair, then take the trouble to have it well-styled.

● Never compete with others in the attraction stakes. There will always be those who look more beautiful and those less beautiful than you. So what! It's what you make of yourself that matters.

● Whenever appropriate, try to look happy and positive whatever you are feeling. Positive feelings show. They light up those around you – and reflect back on you too.

And, of course, how you behave when you meet people will be crucial to the reception you get. So it is important to pay attention to what messages you send out through your body language when you meet someone:

● The way we walk, stand and sit sends out dramatic signals about our level of confidence. Keep your body upright, and avoid slouching. Hold yourself in a poised way without looking too stiff.

- Where you look also matters and so do your gestures. A downward gaze or a lack of eye contact shows uneasiness, as do fidgeting and crossed arms. Look warmly at the person with whom you are talking. Make eye contact in a friendly non-threatening way and respond with interest and animation. Face the person you are talking with, making him or her feel like the only person in the room with you even when you are surrounded by others.

- Once you have joined in with other people, forget about how you look and get on with enjoying the occasion.

- Take a real interest in what you are doing, be enthusiastic, and show interest in others around you.

- Don't put yourself down. If someone compliments you, resist the urge to respond with a self-deprecating remark (eg: 'oh, this old shirt… I've had it for years' ). Instead, just smile warmly and say 'thank you'.

In summary, attractiveness, as you can see and probably know, is much more about how we behave than what we look like. There is more about how to manage other people's reactions in Chapter 4.


## 3. Getting the knowledge

It is essential to have clear and correct information about your skin condition in order to manage the condition well and to maintain your skin health in the best way – and be able to explain it to other people too.

Equipping yourself with the best possible information must include as a first priority the help and advice of a qualified medical practitioner. The first stop will be your general practitioner (GP). If the advice and information from your GP is sufficient to manage your condition, that is fine, but do remember that you are entitled under the Patient's Charter to ask for a referral to see a consultant dermatologist if you consider that you need more help. The waiting time to see a consultant can be longer than you would like.

When attending a medical appointment, it can sometimes be easy to get flustered and forget to ask certain questions, or misunderstand the information you are given. The *Changing Faces* publication *Talking to Health Professionals about Disfigurement* is a good basic Guide on how to prepare yourself to talk with your specialist. It is important that you ask questions that you are concerned about in relation to your own situation - so go prepared with questions written down to prompt you.

You can arm yourself with some general information about your medical condition in the meantime. Then your medical appointment can focus on questions about your individual needs, and not just be a general explanatory session about the condition. It is important, however, that you get the best, up to date and reliable information.

It is generally true to say that you will get the least reliable information from the following sources:

● well-meaning friends who have heard something about your condition being cured by a certain procedure. You need individual help relevant for you and you alone.

● advertisements to sell a product which can often be disguised as authoritative articles on a medical condition. If you are impressed by something an advertisement claims, discuss it with your medical practitioner before spending money.

● personal pages on the internet which can often be thinly disguised advertisements or the subjective experiences of someone – who is not you.

● out-dated books that describe former treatment methods. Medical knowledge has progressed rapidly over recent years. Conditions for which there were limited treatment in the past now have much improved options.

Ideally your quest for knowledge should be ongoing. New discoveries are being made all the time. The best source of information for your own treatment is always your own qualified medical practitioner, so if you are concerned about something you hear about ask for his or her advice.

General information about your condition is also useful. The best general information can be obtained from the following sources:

● the voluntary organisation related to your own condition (eg: the Vitiligo Society, the National Eczema Society, the Acne

Support Group). If you do not know whether there is such an organisation, contact *Changing Faces* for details.

- up to date medical dictionaries and encyclopaedias. Your local bookshop or library will have these books.
- the Internet. The best way to search for high-quality health information is to access 'evaluated subject gateways'. Here are some examples:

  Patient UK: www.patient.co.uk/
  Healthfinder: www.healthfinder.gov/
  Health in Focus: www.healthinfocus.co.uk/
  NHS Direct: www.nhsdirect.co.uk/
  Self-help UK: www.self-help.org.uk/
  Healthcentre UK: www.healthcentre.org.uk/

- searches at a medical library. Your local library staff will be able to tell you the address of the nearest medical library to which you can get access. If you want the highest quality information and research, you can do this by carrying out a medical search of the relevant medical journals. This will give you a list of the most recent research studies with a brief summary of the findings of each one. You will need to look for recent publications, those of the last five years. Review articles which summarise and discuss the work done generally in the field are particularly useful. If you think a study looks interesting, you can pay a small amount to have the whole article photocopied for your own use only. Most journals are written for health professionals and therefore you may find that medical jargon is used with which you may not be familiar.

## Support groups

Many people find that joining a local (or national) support group can be an excellent source of information, advice and friendship. The Directory of Voluntary and Self-Help Groups and Self-Help Groups will help you discover whether your condition has a support group. Your GP may have a copy, a medical library will have one or your local library will be able to access one for you. You may find information from a national organisation addressing the needs of your particular condition.

The links page on the *Changing Faces* website gives the

names of many national and international organisations addressing disfiguring conditions (www.changingfaces.co.uk).

## Cosmetic surgery

You may be tempted to consider cosmetic surgery as a way of transforming your appearance. There are people who have indeed had surgery and 'never looked back' and have been delighted with the results. There are also those who have been disappointed with the results, or who have found that despite the cosmetic improvements, the quality of their lives has remained unchanged.

If you are thinking about cosmetic surgery as a way of treating or minimising your skin condition, you will need to talk over this option very carefully with your consultant before making a decision. You will need to know what detailed changes to expect and what exactly the operation will involve. Some cosmetic surgery can be funded by the NHS, but otherwise you may have to pay a considerable amount of money for it.

Having discovered exactly how much difference and improvement the operation would make, you will also need to address the issue of whether your life would really be so much better if your skin looked better. It is tempting to think 'Of course it would!' but there are those who have had extensive surgery only to realise that their self-esteem remained low and that they did not immediately become happier with their changed looks. When you perceive yourself as looking unacceptable it is easy to conclude that an acceptable appearance will automatically bring to you what is missing in your life. Sadly this equation does not exist in this simplistic form. Feeling good about yourself involves a deeper realisation of what really matters to you. You may find it helpful to speak to one of the *Changing Faces* Specialists about these issues – please call the office.

## The use of skin camouflage

Skin camouflage is also called cover cream or cosmetic camouflage. There are creams and powders in a wide range of colours designed to conceal or reduce the noticeability of skin features such as vitiligo, scarring or birthmarks. Skin camouflage is one way of influencing the impression made on other people. People use camouflage for all sorts of reasons. Some use it every day, others on special occasions or for work, or just because they like using make-up.

Wearing skin camouflage is a personal choice for men and women of all ages just like choosing whether or not to put on hair gel or wearing jewellery. It takes patience and skill to use it well and you will need to be given training from a specialist in skin camouflage in how to do this and what are the best creams for your complexion.

Skin camouflage is not the same as the widely available products sold as foundation. Camouflage creams stay on your skin longer and contain titanium dioxide to mask discolouration. Camouflage can be worn while playing sport, even swimming, without the need for special application and it will not stain your clothes, nor rub off onto other people if you are hugged. In general, it is not advisable to use camouflage on broken, dry or inflamed skin. A camouflage specialist will be able to advise you on this. Contact addresses of skin camouflage specialist organisations are included in the Appendix.

Some products are available on prescription. Others can be bought at full price. Some people can get the services of a skin camouflage specialist free of charge under the NHS. Otherwise, you will have to pay for your consultation.

## Alternative and complementary therapies

Alternative therapies involve quite literally using an alternative, usually natural way of treating your condition. Complementary treatments work alongside the main orthodox therapies.

Many of these treatments involve the use of herbs and 'natural' substances and procedures which are thought to have healing or restorative functions. Many of the most valuable drugs in medicine today are in fact derived from plants and were originally discovered by chance. And many people claim to have improved skin conditions as a result of alternative or complementary therapies.

Over recent years there has been increasing scientific research linking certain substances to improved conditions. If you hear about a certain type of treatment that is recommended for your own condition, it is best not to be swayed by anything that comes in the form of an advertisement. Instead, contact the voluntary organisation that addresses your particular condition and find out what research has been done to support the claims of the treatment.

In summary, becoming well-informed about your condition and its treatment means that you can exert a certain amount of power over it and can make good decisions about the options that are available. You empower yourself to become the architect of your treatment rather than a passive recipient of advice that may not be appropriate.

## 4. Facing others with confidence

Having a medical skin condition can sometimes make people feel preoccupied with their own appearance, placing a lot of emphasis on their skin. This can mean that they appear rather self-absorbed which can make it difficult for other people in social situations. Managing your future with a medical skin condition means learning how to manage other people's reactions very effectively – by being prepared for them.

### Understanding the SCARED syndrome

We are all identified partly by our faces. We notice other people's faces when we first meet, especially. When we talk with others, it is customary to look at their faces. Much of our attention is directed at a central triangle made by the eyes, nose and mouth, as we gather information about them. Whether or not they smile, look at us directly or glance away can often give us more clues about what they are thinking than the words they say. Our faces are the canvases on which our feelings are painted.

These challenges in social encounters are common to lots of people with different disfigurements and it has been found to be useful to have a way of understanding what can happen to people who are feeling uncomfortable in social situations.

At *Changing Faces*, we have evolved such a model; it is called the SCARED Syndrome, each letter of SCARED standing for an aspect of what can happen when you are feeling 'scared' of being with people.

Someone with a noticeable skin condition may feel and behave 'scared':

| FEELING | | BEHAVIOUR |
|---|---|---|
| self-conscious | **S** | shy |
| conspicuous | **C** | cowardly |
| angry, anxious | **A** | aggressive |
| rejected | **R** | retreating |
| embarrassed | **E** | evasive |
| 'different' | **D** | defensive |

'Scared' behaviour may also appear in the people who are facing the person with a medical skin condition. They can sometimes behave in ways that you find hurtful or unacceptable. They may stare at you, make offensive comments, offer advice, avoid eye contact or even ignore you. Or they may be excessively sympathetic. Other people can feel and behave 'scared' too:

| FEELING | | BEHAVIOUR |
|---|---|---|
| sorry, shocked | **S** | staring, speechless |
| curious, confused | **C** | clumsy |
| anxious | **A** | asking, awkward |
| repelled | **R** | recoiling, rude |
| embarrassed | **E** | evasive |
| distressed | **D** | distracted |

## Taking the initiative and gaining confidence

This SCARED Syndrome can be extremely frustrating to be in – but the good news is that there are many ways to deal with it. The most effective ways have been found to involve the person with the medical skin condition 'taking the initiative'. Instead of waiting for the other person to react to your condition, you take the first steps in a pro-active way.

*Changing Faces* has developed a way of storing and bringing to mind a range of ways to take the initiative that will help you to manage all kinds of social situations.

REACH OUT is a 'tool box' of principles for initiative-taking behaviour.

### R - Reassurance

If people seem to be staring at you, you can break the tension by smiling, nodding or making a neutral but pleasant remark. For example, in a long supermarket queue, a person with a medical skin condition may turn to someone else and smile, perhaps adding that the shop appears particularly busy. This helps the other person see that you are a person behind the looks. It also gives you both permission to look at each other in a more natural manner, and feel more comfortable together.

### E - Energy and effort

Energy and effort are often needed to create a good impression: for example, having the energy to speak up to get someone's attention, keep it, and get what is wanted from the situation, rather than being dominated by others. You can generate your own energy by raising the speed or volume of your speech or using more active body language.

### A - Assertiveness

Being assertive involves deciding what you want, and whether it is reasonable, then asking for it directly and politely. Being prepared for the situation helps. It is important to bear in mind that others have the right to disagree or refuse a request. Being aggressive or manipulative is not assertive behaviour – it can be a sign of poor social skills and produce bad results.

# R E A C H

### REASSURANCE

involves getting in first, letting the other person know you are human with a brief remark, a nod or a wink.

### ENERGY AND EFFORT

are needed to tell the other person, that you are worth spending time with.

### ASSERTIVENESS

means being quite clear about what you want, and saying it effectively.

### COURAGE

means tackling the future; taking one step at a time to face the situations you find difficult, and focusing on your positive achievements.

### HUMOUR

is one of your most effective tools. Making a situation more light hearted helps other people to approach you.

# O U T

### OVER THERE

means changing the subject, and shifting the attention away from your appearance on to something that interests everybody.

### UNDERSTANDING

other people find it difficult to deal with anything that is new to them. If people seem uncertain, don't assume that they are hostile. They may be wondering how to approach you.

### TRY AGAIN

sometimes situations don't go well. Don't give up. Try to understand how you could have managed things differently, and have another go.

### C - Courage

Courage is important in two ways; having the courage to tackle a situation such as a job interview in the first place, and then having courage to talk to yourself in a positive way without allowing negative thoughts such as self-doubt take control. Such positive self-talk can include statements such as: 'People may stare at my vitiligo and wonder what happened to me, but I will have the courage to go beyond that, and be me' or 'I have loads to offer even though my skin looks unusual'. It can take practice to say these things convincingly to yourself and actually mean them, but such self-talk can be practised in progressively more difficult situations for more success.

### H - Humour

Humour can be one of the best ice-breakers when you meet others. It can defuse tension and if people see that you can take control and laugh at yourself, others are more likely to laugh alongside you. Black humour is not to everyone's liking but when an opportunity arises to add a light-hearted comment, it will definitely warm those around you.

### O - Over there

You may well not want to discuss your skin condition with everyone who shows interest. Being assertive means having a right to choose when and if your skin becomes the subject of conversation. So changing the subject in a conversation is a valuable tool to keep control. Learning how to shift the subject of the conversation by asking a question related to a new subject, for example, can give you more control over social situations.

Consciously focusing on people and things outside yourself reduces any self-conscious feelings you may have and keeps you more in touch with what is happening around you. In showing interest in other people you will appear more interesting and attractive yourself. One of the other *Changing Faces* publications may be worth asking for: *Meeting new people, making new friends*.

### U - Understanding

It can be difficult to excuse rude behaviour, but it is important to recognise that people do not usually stare out of malice; more likely, they are curious and do not understand the effect they are having. In public places such a trains, especially, people spend a lot of time staring vaguely ahead, lost in thought. It is easy to imagine that these thoughts are hostile, when eyes meet. It can help to accept that it is likely that people will stare at any appearance that is different, rather than to treat every encounter as a challenge to your dignity and self-esteem.

### T - Try again

When an encounter goes wrong, it can be difficult to summon the courage to have another go. Practice makes perfect, as the saying goes, and everyone makes mistakes along the way. It is useful to think rationally about why things failed. Then steps can be taken to try again, perhaps adapting behaviour next time.

The more you practise these REACH OUT strategies, the better you will manage other people's reactions and the more at ease you will feel in social situations…

Preparing how you will use REACH OUT in particularly challenging situations can be useful as you can adapt the appropriate strategies for maximum effect.

## Talking about your skin

Many people will want to know about your medical skin condition. But you need not feel obliged to discuss it in great detail with everyone you meet, but it is useful to have some ideas to draw on, when and if the subject arises.

The subject is best brought up in an emotionally neutral situation. It is often best if you refer to your condition lightly and briefly, reassuring your friends that your condition is under control medically and that you are managing well. If your condition is transmissible, you will have to describe the necessary barriers. Otherwise, you can be up front about it not being contagious.

Use positive comments where you can – and be assertive if necessary. If you use words such as 'unfortunately' or 'incurable' then people may feel sorry for you. Do you really want that? You will probably find that if you do not describe your skin as a big problem then others will not see it at such either. You will be admired for your directness and coping skills.

Courage may be needed at times, perhaps if your social circle includes people who habitually kiss and hug each other when meeting and leaving. It is also something you will need to have if you want to start a physically close relationship with a special person.

In summary, being prepared for how other people are likely to behave and developing your REACH OUT skills will help you to feel more confident in all social situations. And you will gain the positive feedback from others that will make you feel good about yourself too.

## 5. Sources of help

There are hundreds of medical skin conditions, and many of these can be helped by specific organisations. Below are listed some of the organisations associated with the more common conditions. If your condition is not listed below, see Chapter Three on finding out about medical conditions.

### Acne Support Group
Tel: 020 8841 4747 (Mon-Fri 09.00-17.00)
Website: www.m2w3.com/acne
*Support, advice and information to those affected by acne or rosacea.*

### British Allergy Foundation
Helpline: 020 8303 8583 (Mon-Fri 09.00-17.00)
Website: www.allergyfoundation.com
*Patient information service for people with all types of allergies including skin allergies.*

### British Association of Dermatologists
Tel: 020 7383 0266
Website: www.bad.org.uk
*Fact sheets on general dermatological conditions.*

### Changing Faces
Tel: 020 7706 4232 (Mon-Fri 09.00-17.00)
Website: www.changingfaces.co.uk
*Emotional and practical help for adults, children, families and professionals about any disfigurement.*

## Debra
Helpline: 01344 771961 (Mon-Fri 09.00-17.00)
Website: www.debra.org.uk
*Helps people with epidermolysis bullosa and researches cures.*

## Hairline International – the Alopecia Patients' Society
Tel: 01564 775281 (Mon-Fri 09.00-16.30)
*Help, support and advice to people with alopecia and all hair loss conditions.*

## Herpes Viruses Association (SPHERE) and Shingles Support Society
Helpline: 020 7609 9061 (24-hour message service)
Website: www.herpes.org.uk
*Treatment, information and self-help tips for those suffering from shingles, cold sores and herpes-related viruses.*

## Ichthyosis Support Group
Tel: 01635 253829 (Mon-Fri 13.00-20.00)
Tel: 020 7461 0356 (Mon-Fri 20.00-22.00)
Website: www.ichthyosis.co.uk
*Promotes the welfare of children and adults affected by ichthyosis.*

## Lupus UK
Helpline: 01708 731251 (Mon-Fri 09.00-17.00)
Website: www.geocites.com/Hotsprings/2911/
*Advice, help and support to people affected by lupus, including the condition discoid lupus.*

## National Eczema Society
Helpline: 0870 271 3604 (Mon-Fri 13.00-16.00)
Website: www.eczema.org
Also: www.skincarecampaign.org
*Support and advice to people with eczema.*

## National Lichen Sclerosus Support Group (UK)
Website: www.hiway.co.uk/lichensclerosus
*Information and support about lichen sclerosus.*

### Neurofibromatosis Association
Helpline: 020 8547 1636 (Mon-Fri 09.00-17.00)
Minicom: 020 8392 0184
Website: www.nfa-uk.org.uk
*Supports, advises and helps people affected by neurofibromatosis.*

### Psoriasis Association
Helpline: 01604 711129 (Mon-Fri 09.00-17.00)
Website: www.timewarp.demon.co.uk/psoriasis.html
*Advice, help and support to people suffering from psoriasis.*

### Raynaud's & Scleroderma Association
Tel: 01270 872776 (Mon-Fri 09.00-17.00)
Freephone message service: 0800 917 2494
Website: www.raynauds.demon.co.uk
*Information and support to people affected by Raynaud's and scleroderma.*

### Vitiligo Society
Helpline: 020 7840 0855 (Mon-Fri 10.00-17.00)
Freephone helpline:  0800 018 2631 (Mon-Fri 10.00-17.00)
Website: www.vitiligosociety.org.uk
*Information, help and support for people with vitiligo.*

### XP Support Group
Helpline: 01494 890981 (Mon-Fri 09.00-21.00)
Website: www.//xpsupportgroup.org.uk
*Support, help and information to those affected by xeroderma pigmentosum and other photosensitive conditions.*


## Skin camouflage specialists:

### British Association of Skin Camouflage
25 Blackhouse Drive, Silkstone Common, Barnsley, S Yorks D75 4SD
Tel: 01226 790744

### British Red Cross Skin Camouflage Service
National Headquarters, 9 Grosvenor Crescent, London SW1 7EJ
Tel: 020 7235 5454